Teaching Disco Square Dancing to Our Elders: A Class Presentation

By

LARISSA FASTHORSE

Original music

by

BRIAN JOSEPH

Dramatic Publishing

Woodstock, Illinois • Australia • New Zealand • South Africa

*** **NOTICE** ***

IMPORTANT BILLING AND CREDIT REQUIREMENTS

All producers of the play *must* give credit to the author of the play and the composer of the music in all programs distributed in connection with performances of the play and in all instances in which the title of the play appears for purposes of advertising, publicizing or otherwise exploiting the play and/or a production. The names of the author and composer *must* also appear on a separate line, on which no other name appears, immediately following the title, and *must* appear in size of type not less than fifty percent (50%) the size of the title type. Biographical information on the author and composer, if included in the playbook, may be used in all programs. *In all programs this notice must appear:*

"Produced by special arrangement with
THE DRAMATIC PUBLISHING COMPANY of Woodstock, Illinois"

Teaching Disco Square Dancing to Our Elders: A Class Presentation was originally developed and produced by Native Voices at the Autry in Los Angeles. The world premiere was given February 8, 2008, at the Autry National Center. Executive producers: Jean Bruce Scott and Randy Reinholz. The cast was as follows:

Kenny Two Hawks . . . . Noah Watts

Martin Leads to Water . . . . Robert Vestal

Amanda Smith . . . . Tonantzin Carmelo

Grandma Two Hawks . . . . Lavonne Rae Andrews

Directed by José Cruz González with scenic design by Susan Scharpf, lighting design by Leigh Allen and costume design by Christina Wright. Original music by Brian Joseph and choreography by Larissa FastHorse.

Teaching Disco Square Dancing
to Our Elders:
A Class Presentation

CHARACTERS

KENNY TWO HAWKS: 14, Lakota. The wise-cracking ringleader and Martin's best friend. Although about to fail out of school, his nonchalance covers his fears.

MARTIN LEADS TO WATER: 14, Lakota. The sidekick who wants to be something more, but is afraid of losing what little he has.

AMANDA SMITH: 14, half Dakota, half white. The awkward girl whom everyone picks on, even if they aren't sure why, who desperately wants to belong somewhere.

GRANDMA TWO HAWKS: 63, Lakota. The cool grandma who is an elder, but certainly not elderly.

PLACE: Winner, South Dakota. A small border town near the Rosebud Sioux Reservation.

TIME: Present day, end of the school year.

NOTE ON PRODUCTION

This play is a musical of ideas. Although it is not a musical in the traditional singing and dancing sense, the flow and use of the music throughout the piece should be explored with transitions that blend and tie the scenes together.

Part One: Disco

SCENE ONE

*(The street outside middle school, Thursday afternoon.
KENNY TWO HAWKS and his best friend, MARTIN
LEADS TO WATER, rush onto stage. Each is carrying a
large, thin coffee table-style book, half wrapped in paper. MARTIN stops.)*

MARTIN. Kenny, stop. Your topic isn't as bad as mine.

*(KENNY is antsy and frustrated. He tends to have the
energy of a caged animal. He rips the paper off his book
and crumples it angrily.)*

KENNY. It's way worse than yours, but I don't care because I was never going to high school anyway.

*(KENNY tosses his book across the stage. MARTIN is
used to KENNY's outbursts. MARTIN picks up the
book.)*

MARTIN. Sure you are. You're gonna be the first one in
your family to graduate from—
KENNY. Shut up, Martin. I'm flunking and…know what?
I don't care.

MARTIN *(covering his hurt)*. Yes you do. And you're not flunking, you're on the cusp.

KENNY *(disbelieving)*. Cusp? Seriously, if I have to say "cusp" to get into high school, I'm not going.

MARTIN. If you pass this final project, you're in. They'll have to move you up. I'm not going to high school without you. Come on, Kenny, three days, one last project in middle school…

KENNY. I'm not spending my three-day weekend doing a stupid presentation.

MARTIN. Mrs. MacNamera said we could combine projects. We'll do ours together and make it less lame.

KENNY. Tell me how doing a presentation on "Do It Yourself *Disco* Dancing" can't be lame?!? Then combine it with…what did you get?

(MARTIN holds out his book. Dejected.)

MARTIN. *Teaching Square Dancing to Senior Citizens.*

(Suddenly KENNY bursts out laughing. It's like an emotion switch has been flipped. MARTIN brightens, he's been waiting for this.)

KENNY. Know what? This is going to be classic. Kenny Two Hawks and Martin Leads to Water are going to finish middle school with a disco square dance for old people! They'll be talking about us for years.

MARTIN *(hesitates)*. Are we using actual old people? Not my grand—

KENNY. Heck no. Your grandparents are…well…you know. We'll get my Grandma Two Hawks to help us.

MARTIN. She doesn't like being called old. I don't think sixty-three is technically even a senior citizen anymore.
KENNY. So we make her act elderly. She's cool. She'll do it.

(MARTIN glances through their books. He becomes concerned.)

MARTIN. Um…there's another problem here.
KENNY. What?
MARTIN. You need couples for this. Like girls.
KENNY. So you dance with Grandma and I'll like…give the presentation thing. You know the MC and DJ.
MARTIN. No way! I'm not going to be the only one disco square dancing with your grandma. *(He is mad. KENNY can see it, but he still tries.)*
KENNY. The senior citizen part is yours…I didn't care about high school anyway…
MARTIN *(pulls out his big guns)*. So you're gonna take the job at the hog farm with your dad?
KENNY *(warning)*. You really want to bring our dads into this, 'cause I'm locked and loaded, Martin.
MARTIN. You're not making me do this one alone, Kenny.

(KENNY knows this look, MARTIN's not budging. KENNY gives him this one. He glances back toward the school.)

KENNY. Which girl? *(Counts off with various memories.)* Marla, Jessica, Courtney, Sasha and Sunrise aren't speaking to me, which means none of their friends are speaking to me. There's Melissa, but I'm not speaking to her.

MARTIN. You have serious issues with girls.

KENNY. OK, let's use your girlfriend, wait…you don't have one. *(Unsure.)* Hold it, isn't there someone else?

MARTIN. Um…I don't think the Mormon missionary girl is allowed to dance. Wait, we are missing someone…

KENNY. There's only forty kids in our whole class…

(There seems to be someone, but they can't put their finger on it. Offstage they hear a whining voice.)

AMANDA *(offstage)*. Pleeeease, Mrs. MacNamera. I caaan't. I'll do anything. Give me two other books. I'll do them both. Pleeease.

KENNY & MARTIN. Amanda.

MARTIN. I can't believe we forgot her. That's kind of sad.

KENNY. She's just so…forgettable…and beige.

MARTIN. It's not her fault she's a mixed breed.

KENNY. I didn't mean her skin color. She's beige all through.

MARTIN. But she is a girl, and she needs some help. We should see what she's got.

KENNY. I don't know…

(AMANDA SMITH stumbles onto stage, trips and drops her book. It tumbles across the floor to MARTIN's feet. He picks it up and shows the title to KENNY. Interesting.)

MARTIN *(to KENNY)*. We can totally do this one.

KENNY. You understand one of us has to dance with her? I'm just thinking of our safety.

(MARTIN gives AMANDA her book back. She is upset, but already trying to fade into the background. We can almost see the beige filling her.)

MARTIN. What's up? You got a problem with your presentation topic?

AMANDA. Um…sort of…yeah. I can't…I mean…no.

(She starts to flee off stage. MARTIN urges KENNY to stop her. KENNY turns on his KENNY charm and grabs the book out of her hands.)

KENNY. *Exploring Your Culture: Taking Oral Histories.* That's easy. It's like a report on your grandparents, right?

AMANDA. Yeah, but I don't have any grandparents and even if I did, they aren't…my culture. *(Pained.)* It's mean to make someone do a final presentation on something they don't have. Especially this weekend…

KENNY. So, ask you parents. What's the big deal?

(AMANDA looks at KENNY then bursts into tears. Whoa, not what the guys expected. KENNY looks at her like she's and alien. He abandons AMANDA and joins MARTIN off to the side.)

KENNY. What the heck? We can't work with this.

MARTIN. Come on, Kenny, that wasn't cool.

(They look to AMANDA who's still crying.)

KENNY. What? I don't get—
MARTIN. You know she's adopted. Her parents are the white couple who own the coffee shop. She's half Lakota and half white. They're nice people, but I doubt they know much about Lakota culture.
KENNY. She hangs out with the white kids though, right? I mean she can do white culture, whatever that is.

(AMANDA still crying...)

MARTIN. She doesn't hang out with anybody. Amanda tried to take traditional dancing with the Lakota girls and Courtney totally called her out as a wannabe and she left the class crying, *(AMANDA wails)* like that.
KENNY. That's not cool. Hey, Amanda. I'm sorry. I forgot that you're...you know.

(AMANDA stops crying and starts to go. (KENNY and MARTIN both rush to stop her.)

KENNY. Wait. Here's the deal. Martin and I need another girl for our presentation, and you need...help. My grandma is part of our thing and she's Lakota and knows all the traditional culture and stuff.
MARTIN. We'd all be helping each other.

(AMANDA gets a glimmer of hope, but she's still suspicious.)

AMANDA. You mean your grandma would let me interview her and teach me about Lakota culture? With you guys? Really?
MARTIN. Yeah. We'd be a team.
AMANDA. You think she'd teach me how to dance?
KENNY. Actually, funny thing…our presentation is all about dancing.
AMANDA. Really? That would be sooo incredible! But… we only have three days. Is that enough time? I've never danced…

(KENNY reels her in. MARTIN realizes KENNY is really going to do this.)

KENNY. No way? You'll totally get this. It's easy.
MARTIN. High school, here we come!
KENNY. Tomorrow morning, my basement. OK, Amanda?
AMANDA. All weekend?
MARTIN. Yeah. We'll do one part of the project each day. OK?
AMANDA. Um…I guess…yeah. I can't believe you guys are doing this with me.
KENNY. Believe it, girl. We're going to totally rock "Teaching Disco Square Dancing to Our Elders: A Class Presentation"!
MARTIN & KENNY. Bye, Amanda!

(The guys take off.)

AMANDA *(confused)*. Disco square dancing? Wait— *(She's alone. She goes the other way.)*

SCENE TWO

(Thursday evening. AMANDA tucks into a corner of the stage, speaking quietly into a phone. She's somewhere in her house.)

AMANDA. I need to leave a message for room 14— No no no. I don't want to talk to her— Tell her her daughter— No, just say Amanda called and, tell her I'm sorry she came all this way but I don't know if I can... I won't be home all weekend so please, please don't call here...my house. I'll call back later. *(She hangs up, looking guilty.)*

SCENE THREE

(KENNY and MARTIN enter KENNY's basement. It's a pretty simple room with a couple chairs, some discarded stuff and a boombox. Nothing fancy.)

KENNY. You saw her walking here. Why didn't you wait for her?

MARTIN. I figured she could walk by herself. Besides... it's Amanda.

KENNY. Didn't know you cared so much about social suicide.

MARTIN. That's mean.

KENNY. You're the one who wouldn't walk with her and now I'm wasting a perfectly good school free Friday waiting for her.

MARTIN. You'd just be sleeping.

(AMANDA runs in.)

KENNY. Why'd it take you so much longer to walk here than Martin?

AMANDA *(immediately intimidated)*. Huh? How do you know?

MARTIN. I saw you. What way did you go?

AMANDA *(very uncomfortable)*. I…I like to go around the park.

MARTIN. First Ave's way faster.

AMANDA. I…I don't mind…

KENNY. Tomorrow you walk with Martin. *(MARTIN shoots KENNY a glare.)* We can't wait for her all day.

AMANDA *(brightens)*. OK. That's cool. Should we meet or…

KENNY. It's not a date. Just find him and walk.

(AMANDA feels foolish. MARTIN sees it.)

MARTIN. I'll wait for you at the corner of First and Maple.

KENNY *(yelling)*. Grandma!

(GRANDMA TWO HAWKS enters. She isn't happy.)

GRANDMA TWO HAWKS. Don't push it, Kenny. I'm still recovering from the fact that when you need old, the first person you think of is me.

KENNY. No, Grandma. We thought of Martin's grandparents first, but…you know. *(She nods.)* Amanda's grandparents are so old they're dead. Great-Grandma lives on the rez and neither of us will dance with Great-Grandpa Stone.

MARTIN. I'd rather flunk.

KENNY. So, you were the only one left.

MARTIN. We know you're totally not old enough to be a senior citizen, but we figured you're sooo talented that you could act old.

KENNY *(reluctantly pulls his ace).* Truth is…if I don't do this, they're not letting me to go high school…if I want to go.

GRANDMA TWO HAWKS. You're going. I didn't spend the last nine years dragging your butt into school so that you can work on a hog farm. Unless someone's going to pay you to sit on that wall with those boys?

KENNY. The point is…I've agreed to do this thing so you should be supportive. Besides, you like Martin; do it for him.

(GRANDMA wants to say so much more, but she turns her attention to MARTIN.)

GRANDMA TWO HAWKS. Martin can speak for himself. At least he should. *(Looks to AMANDA.)* How'd they rope you into this?

(AMANDA immediately tries to turn up her beige under the sudden attention.)

AMANDA. I wasn't going to do it, but I…um…they said you'd teach me about your…sort of my…culture.

GRANDMA TWO HAWKS. Your parents are Mark and Sarah Smith, right? *(AMANDA nods.)* They are good people.

AMANDA. Yes, ma'am.

GRANDMA TWO HAWKS. Oh for heaven's sake. Don't start ma'aming me. Call me Grandma, everyone does. Even though I'M NOT OLD.

MARTIN. Not even close.

GRANDMA TWO HAWKS. What do you need me to do?

(KENNY pulls out his disco book.)

KENNY. We're starting with the disco part today since that's going to be the hardest. Here. *(He hands the book to GRANDMA. She refuses to take it.)*

GRANDMA TWO HAWKS. You're kidding, right? *(Acting elderly.)* Besides, I don't think my poor old eyes can read that thing.

KENNY. Nobody likes a sarcastic grandma.

GRANDMA TWO HAWKS. I've got *Idol* TiVoed. Call me when you've done your work.

(GRANDMA smiles and leaves. AMANDA halfheartedly calls after her.)

AMANDA. But, what about my part?

KENNY. Fine. I'll drop the book on the floor and we'll learn whatever page falls open. Let fate decide. *(He drops the book and picks it up.) The Lover's Swing?* "This is an intimate step for couples."

(They stand there in awkward silence. KENNY and MARTIN glance at AMANDA. She turns red.)

KENNY. That doesn't sound like Grandma. *(Pages through.)* They have line dances. Old people like those, right? This one's called the Bus Stop. Martin, figure this out.

MARTIN. Nuh-uh. The disco part is all you. I'll be taking a break over here.

KENNY. Whatever. You probably couldn't do it anyway.

(KENNY goes to one side of the stage with his book to figure out the Bus Stop. MARTIN goes to the other side of the stage and chills.

AMANDA stands in the middle, apparently forgotten. She chooses MARTIN and joins him. It's awkward. AMANDA finally speaks up.

Through all of this, KENNY is lamely working out a dance.)

AMANDA. So what's with your grandparents?

MARTIN. The drunk ones or the mean ones?

AMANDA. Oh. It's none of my business.

MARTIN. No, it's OK. Everyone knows. *(To KENNY.)* Hey, Kenny, what's up with my grandparents?

KENNY. The drunk ones or the crazy ones?

MARTIN *(to AMANDA)*. Forgot crazy. It all overlaps. The drunk ones are nice as long as they're drunk, but then they're crazy. The mean ones aren't drunk anymore or never get drunk but are also crazy. So, I guess it all comes down to crazy.

AMANDA. Sorry. What about your folks?

(MARTIN considers her while KENNY flounders with his book.)

MARTIN. You know, when I was a kid I used to imagine that one day my real family would show up, say I was adopted by mistake and take me back. That would have been the best day of my life.

AMANDA. Maybe not. Didn't you ever think they could have been worse?

MARTIN. No…'cause I made them up. Why would I imagine them worse?

KENNY *(yelling)*. Grandma! *(To MARTIN and AMANDA.)* Try to keep up.

(KENNY starts a disco song. They try to follow KENNY's best John Travolta imitation. The kids start to get the dance and have some fun.

GRANDMA TWO HAWKS enters the basement, skeptical. The boys take the fun too far. They goof around, becoming complete disco chaos. GRANDMA is disappointed.)

GRANDMA TWO HAWKS. You've learned disco in fifteen minutes?

KENNY. It's not like it's deep.

GRANDMA TWO HAWKS. Why?

KENNY. Why what?

GRANDMA TWO HAWKS. Why do disco? Why dance at all?

(They all stop. KENNY is annoyed.)

KENNY. 'Cause they're making me, and Martin wouldn't help with—
GRANDMA TWO HAWKS. Not good enough. When you understand why, call me. *(Gives them the evil eye.)* Not until then. I've got to braid my hair for a lunch at the bingo hall.

(KENNY is over it. He tosses the book across the room.)

KENNY. Can't she give me a break? I mean it's disco, who cares?
MARTIN. Obviously Grandma does.

(The three kids stand around, at a loss for what to do next. AMANDA checks the time, nervous.)

AMANDA. I need to make a phone call.
KENNY. It's upstairs. *(AMANDA whimpers and escapes. KENNY is still frustrated.)* She's a drain.
MARTIN. We'll need her. Besides, we can't dump her now.
KENNY. We may regret this.
MARTIN. What part of Teaching Disco Square Dancing to Our Elders did you plan not to regret?
AMANDA *(calling from upstairs)*. Martin, phone!

(MARTIN takes off, leaving KENNY with his book. He starts reading. AMANDA returns. She is nervous around KENNY.)

AMANDA. I didn't get to use the phone. Because it rang for Martin.

KENNY. Thrilling.

AMANDA. So I'll have to go back and use it…after Martin's done.

KENNY. Thanks for keeping me posted.

(AMANDA gives up. MARTIN returns, he looks seriously bummed out, but he tries to act casual.)

MARTIN. Hey, I've got to crash here.

KENNY. The folks?

MARTIN. Yeah.

KENNY. OK. I've gotta make a call. It may take a while so why don't we take an early lunch break? See ya.

AMANDA *(annoyed)*. I really need to call…I wish I had a cell phone. *(AMANDA wants to go, but MARTIN looks really rattled.)* Um…is something wrong?

MARTIN. They're having a party and don't want me around for a couple days.

AMANDA *(shocked)*. A couple days?!? They can't do that. You can't just kick your kids out for a party.

MARTIN. Trust me, it's better than being there. When they have these parties…things happen. I just wish my little sister wasn't there. *(MARTIN gets very dark. This is really troubling him.)*

AMANDA. Cassie in seventh, right? Why doesn't she get kicked out too?

MARTIN. 'Cause that girl can drink like a man. They don't mind her. But sometimes Kenny and I have been able to sneak her out early. If she's not with them, she won't do it.

(AMANDA struggles to be brave. She pushes through her natural beige.)

AMANDA. Then let's go get her. I'll…come…with you.

MARTIN. Thanks, but if my dad comes after us, you won't be much help.

AMANDA *(her head is reeling)*. We should go get Kenny.

MARTIN. Naw. He's gonna go hang out with the guys on the highway for a while. I don't like to bother him there.

AMANDA. Bother him? I thought he was your best friend.

MARTIN. He is, but we have stuff we do separate.

AMANDA. But, we're working, and he just left you when he must know—

MARTIN. Shut up, Amanda. Kenny's been my best friend all my life. You just showed up, so you don't get to say anything about him. He's got his own problems. He'll be back in a while and we'll get this thing done.

AMANDA. But—

MARTIN. He's not using the phone. He was just messing with you. Go make your call.

(MARTIN has his serious face on again. AMANDA gives up and goes, but she feels horrible.

MARTIN kicks a chair over. He paces, frustrated. Suddenly he makes a decision and takes off.)

SCENE FOUR

(A couple hours later. KENNY runs into the basement, calling back off stage. He tosses his book on a chair.)

KENNY. Get your lazy butts back down here!

(AMANDA and MARTIN enter. MARTIN drops a duffle bag in the corner.)

KENNY. Jeez. That was like a two-hour lunch. We've got serious disco work to do here. *(Yelling.)* Grandma!
AMANDA. Good. Maybe I could ask her some questions.
KENNY. Your part's Sunday.
AMANDA. I know, but just in case.
KENNY. Just in case what?
AMANDA. Nothing.
MARTIN *(to KENNY)*. Do you know why we disco?
KENNY. Check it out. *(Yelling.)* Grandma!

(GRANDMA enters, more skeptical than ever. She stays on the edge of the stage. KENNY picks up his book and dramatically opens to a page.)

GRANDMA TWO HAWKS. So…
KENNY *(reading)*. "Disco formed from generations of music and social dances. From the cha-cha to the tango to rock to soul, disco brought together many influences in a new way that hadn't been seen before." It's a mixed-breed movement…like Amanda.

(AMANDA isn't sure what to think of his comment, but she and MARTIN are impressed with KENNY's answer. GRANDMA considers KENNY.)

GRANDMA TWO HAWKS. Is that all?

KENNY. I've got another line dance. It's a little tricky, but we'll do it, then you can ask questions.

(KENNY hits the music. Before he can lead the first step, GRANDMA TWO HAWKS jumps in front of the kids and leads a very funky New Yorker. It's pure '70s disco. The kids stop and stare, shocked. GRANDMA finishes.)

GRANDMA TWO HAWKS. What else you got?

KENNY *(turns the music off)*. What the heck?

MARTIN. You know how to disco dance?

GRANDMA TWO HAWKS. I was around in the '70s. Your grandfather and I would go to Rapid City once a month for the disco competition.

AMANDA. Can we move on to oral history now?

KENNY. Why'd you make me go through all this?

GRANDMA TWO HAWKS. Because that is the assignment, and because you can. You are too smart to be this lazy, Kenny. Your father could have been something, but he's wasting his life with hogs and beer. I will not let that happen to you.

(Her words have a surprisingly strong affect on KENNY. He becomes withdrawn.)

MARTIN. Can you show us more?

GRANDMA TWO HAWKS. Nope. That's your job. But next we're dancing as couples. I'm with Martin. *(To MARTIN.)* And you'd better learn how to lead. *(To AMANDA.)* You're the woman while I'm gone. Don't let them push you around. I'm off to set up concessions for the tractor pull tonight.

(GRANDMA TWO HAWKS takes off. KENNY throws his book across the room, again.)

KENNY. Forget this! I do all this work and she knew? I don't need this. *(He collapses on the floor, drama.)*
AMANDA *(to MARTIN)*. Is he quitting again? We just got back.

(MARTIN shrugs, probably. AMANDA is over this.)

AMANDA. She just wants you to do your own work. We all have to.
KENNY. Don't tell me about my life. You don't know anything.
AMANDA. You're not the boss, Kenny.
KENNY. I'm the boss of disco.
AMANDA. Then do something. Grandma wants a couples' dance.
KENNY. Fine. *(He jumps up. He opens the disco book and hands it to MARTIN. KENNY hits the music.)* Stay close, Martin. Come on, Amanda, let's dance, as a couple.

(KENNY holds his arms open, challenging AMANDA to step close to him. AMANDA is really uncomfortable. MARTIN glances at the page he's holding open.)

MARTIN. Saturday Night Hustle? That sounds kind of hard.

KENNY. I can handle it if you can, Aman-duh.

(Both boys expect AMANDA to flee. MARTIN feels kind of bad.

Surprisingly, AMANDA pulls herself together and steps into KENNY's arms. Interesting. KENNY fights discomfort. MARTIN sees AMANDA in a new light.)

MARTIN. Guess she can.

(KENNY is annoyed. AMANDA grabs him and pulls him close. They struggle through the dance while MARTIN tries to keep the book in view, they all talk at once.)

KENNY. No, it starts like this. Follow me. Can't see, Martin. Etc.

AMANDA. Turn the other way. That's wrong, Kenny. This way. Etc.

MARTIN. Amanda has to see too.

(KENNY dips AMANDA and almost drops her.)

AMANDA. Ah!!

KENNY. This way. Now out, then the turn into me. Into me.

(AMANDA coil turns into KENNY then he spins her away and she falls right into MARTIN's arms.

MARTIN doesn't let her go right away. Their eyes meet. MARTIN is surprised by what he sees in her. AMANDA turns red and stares at the floor.)

MARTIN. You OK?

KENNY. She's fine, just stay out of our dance space.

(KENNY grabs for AMANDA. MARTIN can't quite let go. Something has definitely changed.

Caught between the boys, AMANDA is completely flustered. She backs away.)

AMANDA. I've got to go to…the…I'll be back. *(She flees. MARTIN turns off the music.)*

KENNY. What was that?

MARTIN. She's a klutz. We sort of expected it.

KENNY. No. Grandma trips and I grab her arm. That was all…romantical.

MARTIN. Shut up.

KENNY. It's cool, I mean she is technically a girl, but you've got to be careful. I'd bet money that Amanda Smith's never been kissed by a guy in her life.

MARTIN. Come on. Everyone's played truth or dare. She had to…right?

KENNY. With who? The girl's got no friends. You saw how she just freaked. She's weird and if you're not careful you'll have some crazy stalker girl on your hands for nothing.

MARTIN. Don't talk about her like that.

KENNY. You want to ruin this whole project?

MARTIN *(getting irritated)*. You don't care about it anyway.

KENNY. Right, but I'm doing all of this for you, so—

MARTIN. You only do things for yourself.

KENNY. What does that mean?

MARTIN. You know that Cassie is home, but it's always
about Kenny and his stuff.

KENNY. You want us to go get her? Just ask.

MARTIN. I went back at lunch. Things were…bad already.
My dad wouldn't let me in.

KENNY. So where'd you get the bag?

MARTIN. My aunt left it out. But that's not the point. I
needed you and you were smoking on a wall with a
bunch of losers!

KENNY. Those are my friends!

MARTIN. Then what am I?

*(The boys push into a shoving match. AMANDA rushes
back in the room.)*

AMANDA. He needed you, Kenny.

KENNY & MARTIN. Shut up, Amanda.

AMANDA. I'm trying to help. *(She pushes herself between
the guys.)*

KENNY. This is between me and Martin.

AMANDA. No it's not. This affects my grade too, and
Martin's. And I'm sick of you being so mean.

KENNY. Fine. Disco is OVER! Tomorrow we start square
dancing. Hope you're ready, Martin, 'cause it's all you.

*(KENNY takes off. MARTIN thinks about running after
him, but doesn't. He glares at AMANDA.)*

AMANDA. I'm sorry, I just—
MARTIN. Leave me alone. *(He grabs his bag and goes. He's not chasing, just going.)*
AMANDA. But where will you go?
MARTIN. It's none of your business.

(AMANDA is left alone. Confused, she gets her stuff and heads out.)

AMANDA. I think I was better off alone.

END PART ONE

Part Two: Square Dancing

SCENE ONE

(Saturday morning, the basement. MARTIN and AMANDA enter together. MARTIN stows his duffle bag in the corner. As they talk he sets up two chairs, one UC, one DC.)

AMANDA. Thanks for walking with me this morning. I wasn't sure if we were doing this…after yesterday.

MARTIN. We're friends, we fight sometimes. You know how it is.

AMANDA. Not really. It's kind of stressful to have friends.

MARTIN. I guess. But it's better than nothing.

AMANDA. Yeah. You think we'll be done early again?

MARTIN. Never know. Why?

AMANDA. Maybe I could start on Grandma today. You know, in case.

MARTIN. Why do you keep saying that?

AMANDA *(uncomfortable)*. I may go to a family type thing tomorrow.

MARTIN. You should have told us.

AMANDA. I know. I wasn't…I'm not sure. Don't worry about it. I'm not going.

MARTIN. You sure?

AMANDA. Yeah. Forget it.

(KENNY comes down the stairs. Everyone is a little careful of one another. GRANDMA follows right behind him.)

KENNY *(to GRANDMA)*. For square dancing you show up. I always knew he was your favorite.
GRANDMA TWO HAWKS. Favorite what? Friend of yours? Absolutely. Although you don't give Martin much to compete with.

(She ruffles MARTIN's hair affectionately. MARTIN likes it.)

GRANDMA TWO HAWKS. Truth is, I thought you kids could use a cool bath of Grandma to put out the fires. Besides, you can't do a square dance without couples.
MARTIN *(hopeful)*. Do you know how to do this kind of dancing too?
GRANDMA TWO HAWKS. I've been to a square dance or two.
AMANDA. I've been to some too.
KENNY. Oh my God. You've been to a square—
GRANDMA TWO HAWKS *(warning)*. Kenny…

(KENNY stays quiet. AMANDA gives him a glare. MARTIN puts the book down and hits some fiddle music on the boombox.)

MARTIN. Well, turns out you need four couples for this, 'cause that's why it's called "square." I put the chairs here for the other couples. So, it's pretty easy, just follow me. I'm with Grandma, you guys stand next to each other.

(AMANDA and KENNY reluctantly stand side by side across from MARTIN and GRANDMA.)

MARTIN. Bow to your partner. *(He does the step with GRANDMA. KENNY isn't going for this corny stuff.)* Come on, Kenny. *(KENNY gives in and bows to AMANDA.)* Bow to your corner. That's the chairs. Promenade your partner. *(The others follow and MARTIN leads GRANDMA through the steps.)* Swing. Do-si-do. Seesaw. That's a double do-si-do.
GRANDMA TWO HAWKS. Ladies' chain!

(GRANDMA takes over and reaches across to AMANDA. They do a ladies' chain, exchanging partners.)

MARTIN. Guy's chain! *(The boys think it's funny and rush across to change partners.)* Grand right and left. *(They go around the circle using the chairs as partners. MARTIN and KENNY get goofy. Going faster as they get more confident.)* Star. Faster! Box the gnat. Faster! Swing! Arm turn!

(The boys hook arms and swing each other faster and faster until they fall into a pile on the floor, friends again.

The boys pull each other down, trying to be the first one up.

AMANDA and GRANDMA move to one side. Boys.)

GRANDMA TWO HAWKS. They're useless for a while. When have you been to a square dance?

AMANDA. My mom's family lives on a farm near Watertown. All the neighbors get together and clean out a barn to have a square dance and cookout. They string Christmas lights and have a band. It's corny.

GRANDMA TWO HAWKS. Sounds like fun. Kind of like the socials we had on the reservation when I was a kid. Everyone would come over and drum and sing and have a big open fire with roasting meats. The dancing circle would go on all night.

AMANDA *(enthralled)*. That would be so amazing. I can't imagine.

GRANDMA TWO HAWKS. It's the same thing.

AMANDA. No it's not. Not to me.

(GRANDMA TWO HAWKS is saddened by AMANDA's words. KENNY and MARTIN have finally gotten ahold of themselves.)

MARTIN. I think we've got the basics covered. What happens next is a caller calls out this song-type thing and everyone follows. It's like a code. *(As MARTIN reads slowly all four move around a little, trying to figure out what steps may fit the words.)*
   "Pioneer and the lawmen too,
   The open range is open for you.
   Promenade left as quick as you can.
   Then grand right and—"

(GRANDMA chokes back an emotional moment. MAR-TIN stops.)

MARTIN. What's wrong?

KENNY *(protective)*. You made her do too much, Martin. What do you need, Grandma? *(He turns off the music. GRANDMA waves off his offer of help.)*

GRANDMA TWO HAWKS. Sometimes it still hits me when I hear words like "open range" and "pioneer."

MARTIN. Why?

GRANDMA TWO HAWKS. Kenny's great-great-grandfather tried to file for a land claim. He saw what was coming and figured it was better to get the land in Indian hands than white.

AMANDA *(quietly to KENNY)*. Pen, where's my pen? *(She looks for a pen. KENNY keeps ahold of her while GRANDMA settles into a chair. AMANDA tries to pull away.)* I need to write this down.

KENNY. Be respectful. *(He keeps a grip on AMANDA. She keeps fighting. GRANDMA is lost in memories, or just ignoring her.)*

GRANDMA TWO HAWKS. Of course they turned him down, our people weren't citizens of this country yet. When he fought it, they shipped him off to jail. By the time he got out, it was too late. *(Shakes it off.)* That's enough heavy first thing in the morning. I need to make some calls for the tribal council meeting. We'll do more a little later. *(GRANDMA goes.)*

(AMANDA breaks free of KENNY's grip and scrambles around the basement, trying to find a pen.)

AMANDA. She has something to say and I don't have a pen!

KENNY. Shut up and listen when your elders talk.

AMANDA. Stop treating me like I'm not one of you.

KENNY. You're not. You're totally not as Indian as me or Martin.

(MARTIN can't believe KENNY pulled the race card. AMANDA is stung.)

MARTIN. Leave me out of this.

AMANDA. My birth mother's Lakota.

KENNY. Yeah? Who are your people? Where are they from?

AMANDA. You don't know anything, Kenny.

KENNY. Speak some Lakota for me.

AMANDA. Leave me alone.

KENNY. *Nituktetanhan he? Táku eniciyapi hwo?*

AMANDA. Shut up!

KENNY. I just asked your name. You don't even know that?

AMANDA. Ask my birth mother. She's here in Winner right now sitting at the Buffalo Motel waiting to meet me. You care so much about who I am, you meet her!

MARTIN. Are you serious? You have to go meet her.

AMANDA *(frustrated)*. I have a mom. I love her and I don't need another one and it's none of your business! *(She runs out.)*

MARTIN. Why'd you have to be so mean?

KENNY. She was rude to Grandma.

MARTIN. That stuff you said wasn't cool, Kenny.

KENNY. 'Spose. But how'd I know her bio mom's here? *(Dejected.)* Since she's a girl she probably expects me to apologize or something.

MARTIN. She's getting used to you.

KENNY. Hey look—

MARTIN. I'm going to see if she's OK. *(He leaves. KENNY wanders around, then takes off.)*

SCENE TWO

(An hour later, the basement. AMANDA enters shyly.)

AMANDA. Anyone here? No one answered so I let myself in. *(She's alone. She sits and waits.)*

(MARTIN enters. He's happy to see her. AMANDA's cute when she's not beige.)

MARTIN. Hey.

AMANDA *(embarrassed)*. Oh, hey.

MARTIN. I've been looking for you.

AMANDA. I'm sorry I ran— *(Surprised.)* Really?

MARTIN. I even went all the way around the park.

AMANDA. You did?

MARTIN. Why do you do that? I won't tell anyone. I promise.

(AMANDA is dying to connect with someone, but this is hard.)

AMANDA. Um…know how the football team runs down first before practice? *(MARTIN nods.)* Well…there's that long fence before the park. I…um…one day they… caught me there.

(MARTIN almost doesn't want to know, but it's like a car crash.)

MARTIN. Caught? What do you mean?

AMANDA. They would always tease me when they ran by, but one day they…surrounded me. There wasn't anywhere to go… *(Living in the memory.)* One of them grabbed me…like my…chest. Then he shoved me to another guy and he…put his hands…on my… They were all laughing and kept…um…shoving me from one to the other. I finally got to the end of the fence and ran into the park. They just kept jogging down the street like nothing happened. So I don't go by the fence anymore.

MARTIN *(looks sick)*. That was you?

AMANDA *(horrified)*. People know? *(She gets up to flee. MARTIN jumps up.)*

MARTIN. I heard some guys bragging there was a girl who let the team feel her up on the street. I thought…

AMANDA. So it's funny to them?

MARTIN. It was wrong, what they did. I'm sorry.

AMANDA. You've never teased me or called me stuff. You're not one of them.

MARTIN. Yeah, but…I should have done something.

AMANDA. Well…it's better than drunk, crazy, and mean. I never knew about that.

MARTIN. I don't know. You want to get a pop or something?

AMANDA. In public? Shouldn't we be working?
MARTIN. Can't 'til the others get back. Maybe walk over to Country King?
AMANDA. People might see us.
MARTIN. So? I don't get what's so wrong with you anyway.

(AMANDA would cry if MARTIN wasn't here.)

AMANDA. I don't either.

(MARTIN and AMANDA get up and head to Country King.)

SCENE THREE

(KENNY's basement, later. Square dance music plays. MARTIN and AMANDA finish a square dance while GRANDMA looks on, eating fries.)

MARTIN. Thanks for the help, Grandma.
GRANDMA TWO HAWKS. Thanks for the french fries. Country King always makes the best fries.

(MARTIN stops the music. KENNY enters alone. He isn't crazy about the happy threesome.)

MARTIN. Hey, Kenny, while you were gone Grandma helped us figure out the rest of our square dance. We've got it down.

KENNY. Good for you. You should be a dance teacher, charm all the ladies, like *Dirty Dancing*.

MARTIN. Ha ha. Now, Grandma. According to this book, "After learning to square dance you will feel more alert, sleep better, and feel like you are still a valued member of society." Any chance you're feeling that?

GRANDMA TWO HAWKS *(amused)*. If that was true, the whole world would be square dancing in the streets. But, I do feel energized by you kids and I'll have to stay up later to catch up on the programs I TiVoed this week, so I'll sleep good. How's that?

MARTIN. Good enough for me. The square dancing portion of our presentation is officially done.

GRANDMA TWO HAWKS. Nice work, Martin. I have time for a cocktail at the VFW. See you kids tomorrow.

(GRANDMA leaves. AMANDA puts the chairs back against the wall, getting ready to go. KENNY talks to MARTIN.)

KENNY. Hey, you wanna hang out? There's an old "Baywatch" marathon on TV today.

MARTIN *(awkward)*. I figured you'd go hang out on the wall. It is Saturday.

KENNY. I'm getting kind of sick of those guys. Besides, you and I haven't done anything but school stuff all weekend.

MARTIN. I…um…already have plans.

(KENNY spots AMANDA killing time and glancing at MARTIN.)

KENNY. Seriously? You guys aren't like…dating, are you?

MARTIN & AMANDA *(both jump)*. No.

MARTIN. In fact, we're just going to hang out at Amanda's. You wanna come?

AMANDA. Yeah, come over, Kenny. My parents would love to meet you. We're having a Monopoly tournament.

KENNY. Monopoly with the folks? I don't think so. There's seven hours of chicks in bikinis waiting upstairs.

MARTIN *(torn)*. Maybe I could…

KENNY. Naw. I'm heading over to the wall for a while. See you guys tomorrow.

(KENNY takes off. MARTIN and AMANDA feel bad.)

AMANDA. You want to go with him?

MARTIN. To the wall? Not really. I'd rather go with you. *(He grabs his duffle bag from the corner of the room.)*

AMANDA. Aren't you coming back here?

MARTIN. Um…I don't think so.

AMANDA *(suspicious)*. How're things going at home?

MARTIN. Um… Can I tell you something? Something you can't tell anyone?

AMANDA. Sure.

MARTIN. I'm not going to live at home anymore.

AMANDA. What does that mean?

MARTIN. I'm never going back. I can't stay here in case Kenny's parents tell on me.

AMANDA. So…you're fourteen, where do you go?

MARTIN. Once when Kenny was out of town I slept on the swaying bridge in the playground. It's like a waterbed. Or what I guess a waterbed is like.

AMANDA *(shocked)*. You can't do that. What about Social Services? They can find you a place to stay.

MARTIN. They'll put me in foster care. I'm not doing that again.

AMANDA. But you can't sleep on the kiddie bridge forever. You have to tell someone.

MARTIN. I just did and you said you wouldn't tell.

AMANDA. But this is serious.

MARTIN. No kidding. I'm the one sleeping in the park. Please don't tell. If you…you know…think I'm OK, don't.

AMANDA *(sincere)*. I think you're a lot better than OK.

MARTIN. You too.

(MARTIN awkwardly makes "the arm move." He finally gets his hand to AMANDA's shoulder. It's exciting and weird for each of them. Just as he goes for the kiss, AMANDA jumps and shrieks, full of nervous energy.)

AMANDA. Ahhh…my playhouse! It's in the backyard. I could bring you food and you could come inside when my parents are at work. No one would know.

MARTIN. Really? Are you sure?

AMANDA. It can't be forever, but until you figure something out.

(MARTIN kisses AMANDA quickly. She jumps away immediately.)

MARTIN. You've never been kissed by a guy before, have you?

AMANDA *(embarrassed)*. It's totally obvious, isn't it?

MARTIN. Well, it's kind of hard to do from a foot away.
AMANDA. Yeah.

(AMANDA pulls together all her courage and tries to lean in closer to MARTIN. She's so nervous, and now it's getting more awkward by the moment.

She blindly leans farther in. MARTIN tries to match her lips, and falls on the floor. AMANDA is mortified.)

AMANDA. I'm so lame.
MARTIN. Naw, it's OK. Let's go home.
AMANDA. Seriously? You still want to come?
MARTIN. Can I hold your hand?
AMANDA. I know how to do that one.

(MARTIN holds out his hand. AMANDA takes it the wrong way, like shaking hands. She corrects and they go off holding hands.)

END PART TWO

Part Three: Culture and Oral History

SCENE ONE

(The basement, Sunday morning. GRANDMA is going through a memory box. AMANDA and MARTIN enter.)

MARTIN. Hey, Grandma.
AMANDA. Good morning, Grandma.

(GRANDMA seems lost in memories. The kids sit next to her. AMANDA pulls out a notebook and pen.)

AMANDA. So, Grandma, can we start with your grandparents today? *(Nothing.)* Grandma?
GRANDMA TWO HAWKS. Have you heard of the Native American Graves Protection and Repatriation Act?
AMANDA. No.
GRANDMA TWO HAWKS. It made museums to give back the things they stole. My mom was still alive to see her father's body returned and buried behind her church. That was a good day.
AMANDA. Huh?

(KENNY runs in all jazzed. He's instantly bugged to see them together.)

KENNY. How'd you guys get here so early?

(MARTIN shushes KENNY.)

GRANDMA TWO HAWKS *(to KENNY)*. Good morning, sleeping beauty.

AMANDA. Where had his body been?

GRANDMA TWO HAWKS. In a box in a storeroom at a museum. The clothes we had buried him in were on display behind glass.

AMANDA *(horrified)*. Wait. You mean someone dug him up after he was dead? That's horrible. That's gotta be against the law.

GRANDMA TWO HAWKS. It is now. When you kids bury me, I'm staying there.

KENNY. Don't say that.

GRANDMA TWO HAWKS. I'm not a superhero, Kenny. One day—

KENNY. We don't have to talk about it.

GRANDMA TWO HAWKS. Fair enough. What's next?

(Before AMANDA can ask more, KENNY hits some funky disco on the boombox.)

KENNY. Hey, I found this warm-up thing we're supposed to do before we dance. It starts like—

MARTIN. It's Amanda's day to start her culture and oral history part with Grandma. *(He turns off the music. KENNY is really over this.)*

KENNY. I'm doing this for the presentation, so we need to practice it. *(MARTIN holds his ground.)* How about I'll lead the warm-up and she can ask her questions at the same time? Is that OK with you?

(MARTIN hesitates. AMANDA is bugged, but MARTIN gives in to keep peace.)

MARTIN. Fine. You can do that, right, Amanda?
AMANDA. I guess. If Grandma can.
GRANDMA TWO HAWKS. Whatever you kids tell me to do, I do.
KENNY. Great. *(He starts disco music.)* These are called waist gyrations. Side, side.

(Through the following, KENNY leads them through a series of isolations: torso, head, hips, fingers combinations.

The closer AMANDA gets to getting some info from GRANDMA, the weirder the moves get to throw AMANDA off.)

AMANDA. Grandma, who was the primary teacher of your culture to you?
GRANDMA TWO HAWKS. Do you know our word for adoption?
AMANDA. No. I don't want to talk about that.
GRANDMA TWO HAWKS. *Hunka.* A family by choice. That's very special.
AMANDA. I know. *(Tries to regroup.)* So, was a grandmother your teacher?

(KENNY does fast headrolls, making it hard to talk clearly.)

GRANDMA TWO HAWKS. Everyone is your teacher. Like you kids. *(To KENNY.)* Slow down there. My head could roll off.

AMANDA. Then, tell me what it meant to you to grow up Lakota?

GRANDMA TWO HAWKS. What did it mean to you to grow up Lakota?

(KENNY has them bending all the way forward and back from the waist. Then all the way around with their torsos.)

AMANDA. Nothing.

GRANDMA TWO HAWKS. Really? You never thought about it at all?

AMANDA. Sometimes. *(KENNY starts thrusting his hip around. AMANDA is frustrated.)* But I'm only asking all this because I got this topic. I have to do it. *(KENNY adds a finger flex with circling hips. It's ridiculous AMANDA is over this. She shuts the music off.)* What is this, Kenny? No one dances like that.

KENNY. You listened to Martin when he was the teacher.

GRANDMA TWO HAWKS. That's it, Kenny. You win, I'm old. I need an aspirin. I'll be back. *(She goes.)*

(KENNY stops his isolations, he won. AMANDA is rattled.)

KENNY. Take your time, Grandma.

AMANDA *(to KENNY)*. We're doing this presentation to-morrow. We let you do your thing, let me do mine.

KENNY. We? You're speaking for Martin now?

MARTIN. Come on, Kenny, stop messing around. Let her do it.

KENNY. I'm not stopping her.

AMANDA. Yes you are. I'm giving up everything to be here and you don't care.

KENNY. You wanna meet your bio mom? Then do it!

MARTIN. Shut up, Kenny!

KENNY. Get out of here! Stop whining about her and go!

(MARTIN grabs KENNY, ready to fight.)

AMANDA. I can't!

KENNY *(still mean)*. Why not?

AMANDA. Because I might love her. And then what if my parents don't love me?

(AMANDA melts down, crying. Both guys are affected. KENNY pushes MARTIN to help her.)

MARTIN. I don't know anyone's parents who love them as much as yours. Not mine, anyway.

KENNY. Look, I know this is crazy, coming from me, but maybe you should talk to your folks about…all this.

AMANDA. I just can't. *(Pulls herself together.)* Anyway, can we not talk about this anymore? I really want to fo-cus on this presentation thing and get it done. OK?

MARTIN. Yeah, sure. How can we help?

AMANDA. I'm really worried about my part. I don't have enough.

KENNY. You know, you've got two professional Indian experts here.

AMANDA. Yeah right.

KENNY *(winking at MARTIN)*. Didn't we tell you? Martin and I are opening an Indian Academy.

MARTIN *(infomercial style)*. In three short weeks you can earn your genuine Indian diploma.

(The guys put on some music and go into an old routine.)

KENNY. First we put you in a cage with a lion, a bear and a cougar and see which one eats…ah, chooses you.

MARTIN *(official voice)*. Indian Academy assumes no liability for lost limbs, bite marks or bear snot.

(AMANDA has to smile.)

KENNY. Then we teach you how ride a horse—

MARTIN. A buffalo!

KENNY. Bareback!

MARTIN. Even better.

KENNY. Of course, we expect your full payment up front. Oh! For graduation, instead of those flat hats, everyone wears long black wigs!

(The guys totally crack themselves up, again. AMANDA joins. They laugh together for the first time.)

MARTIN *(to AMANDA)*. Don't ever be one of those wannabe Indians, OK? *(He stops the music.)*

KENNY. What's with them? They walk around the grocery store wearing buckskin, dragging their fringe across the self-serve doughnuts.

(They all crack up again.)

AMANDA. I promise I won't. I don't know about them, but…you've always had "your people." I think a lot of us just want that.
KENNY. That's sad.
MARTIN. Well, you really are one of our "people."
KENNY. Yeah, we'll even let you go to our Indian academy for free.

(It's a sweet moment for AMANDA. The guys quickly kill it.)

MARTIN. Awwww. That's sweet, Kenny.
KENNY. Let's hug it out.

(The guys make like they're going to hug. AMANDA isn't sure what's happening. Suddenly the guys punch each other.)

MARTIN. Shut up, you loser.
KENNY. You were going for it.
MARTIN. Was not.
KENNY. Yeah, right, back to work.

(MARTIN reaches out and touches AMANDA's hand. He realizes what he's doing and pulls away, but KENNY saw.)

KENNY. Sooo…what are we doing here?

AMANDA. I think I'll go up and talk to Grandma alone, if that's OK?

MARTIN. Sure. We'll work out the dance stuff and fill you guys in when you get back. *(AMANDA leaves. MARTIN waits until he's sure she's gone.)* Cool. Cover for me. I gotta go do something.

KENNY. Stay out of it, Martin.

MARTIN. She can't not meet her mom. She'll regret it.

KENNY. It's a bad plan.

MARTIN. She needs help and I want to help her.

KENNY. Why?

MARTIN. She's helping me with some stuff.

KENNY. Like what? Losing your virginity?

MARTIN *(whiplash moment)*. What the heck is wrong with you?

KENNY. I know you are one—

MARTIN. You don't know anything.

KENNY. I'm getting that. Maybe we should watch some "Oprah".

MARTIN. Shut up. Me and Amanda are sort of seeing each other, but you must have figured that out.

KENNY. Yeah, but I wanted my best friend to tell me himself.

MARTIN. Come on, Kenny. We haven't talked about anything real in years.

KENNY. We're not girls, Martin. I'm there for you where it counts.

MARTIN. Not anymore. Being your best friend stinks. You were all I had, but you'd rather spend your life with a bunch of losers on the wall.

KENNY. I quit this stupid presentation!

MARTIN. Enjoy the hog farm.

(That's it. They guys explode into a wrestling match. KENNY quickly gets the upper hand and is just about to punch MARTIN when he stops himself.)

KENNY. Forget you. I'm done. *(He takes off. MARTIN calls after him.)*
MARTIN. Go, leave again! I'm going to help someone who cares. *(He leaves the basement, too.)*

SCENE TWO

(An hour later. AMANDA and GRANDMA enter the basement looking for the boys.)

AMANDA. Thanks for the lunch, Grandma. It helped. I guess the guys are taking a break.

(Suddenly MARTIN rushes in, excited.)

MARTIN. Amanda, what would totally make your life happy?
AMANDA. Red, curly hair?
MARTIN. Really? Uh…not that.
AMANDA. Friends?
MARTIN. No.
AMANDA. To be accepted as a Lakota?
MARTIN. Stop, this is getting depressing. How about…to meet your birth mother and have it all be cool?
AMANDA. Why?

MARTIN. Because I explained everything to her. She's outside waiting to meet you. *(He waits for the reaction. GRANDMA looks worried. AMANDA freaks.)*

AMANDA. Why would you do that?

MARTIN. You wanted to meet her, and—

AMANDA. No I didn't! I trusted you.

MARTIN. You were just freaked, but she totally gets it. She only wants—

AMANDA. I hate you!

MARTIN. But—

AMANDA. Stay out of my life! *(She runs out. MARTIN is completely stunned.)*

MARTIN. I just wanted to help her, Grandma.

GRANDMA TWO HAWKS. Well, her life is about to change forever. Don't you think that should have been Amanda's choice?

MARTIN. But…how could she know she's got another family out there?

GRANDMA TWO HAWKS. Sometimes there isn't a fantasy ending, Martin, I'm sorry.

MARTIN. But if she hates me and Kenny quit, what happens now?

GRANDMA TWO HAWKS. Kenny quit? Quit what?

MARTIN. The presentation. Which means he's quit school.

GRANDMA TWO HAWKS. When did this happen?

MARTIN. This morning.

GRANDMA TWO HAWKS. Why didn't you tell me?

MARTIN. There's been a lot going on.

GRANDMA TWO HAWKS. I've got to go find him. *(She rushes out.)*

MARTIN. But…where do I go now? *(He takes off, dejected.)*

SCENE THREE

(Later. MARTIN knocks on the door of his house.)

MARTIN. I'm home. WAKE UP! Someone let me in. *(Nothing. Something snaps in him. He pounds and kicks at the door.)* YOU CAN'T DO THIS! I WANT TO BE HOME!! PLEASE LET ME IN! *(Still nothing. MARTIN searches, finds a rock and throws it at the house. We hear the sound of a WINDOW BREAKING. MARTIN runs off stage.)*

SCENE FOUR

(Sunday evening on the wall. KENNY sits alone. AMANDA enters. Something is different about her, she's not beige.

KENNY looks around, to be sure they're alone.)

AMANDA. So, this is the wall. *(She sits on the wall next to KENNY. He automatically moves over.)*
KENNY. You need to keep moving.
AMANDA *(not phased by KENNY)*. This is what you do?
KENNY. Pretty much. The guys went for smokes. You gotta be gone when they get back.
AMANDA. I won't take long. Here's the thing. I just met my birth mom and it was totally weird.
KENNY. Sorry.
AMANDA. No, it's OK. Once I calmed down, we sort of just sat there, staring at each other. Then I start think-

ing…and I realize I'm thinking like my mom, my real mom. And I'm moving my hands like my dad. I suddenly get that, no matter what, my parents are my people. And like it or not, you and Martin are my people now, too. So, even though I'm still mad at him, I need your help to help Martin.

KENNY *(concerned)*. What's wrong? Did something happen?

AMANDA. Yeah. His best friend's an idiot. But that's not all…

SCENE FIVE

(Late Sunday night in the basement. MARTIN sleeps across the two chairs. He hears noises and bolts awake as KENNY and AMANDA enter.)

MARTIN. Grandma, I was just waiting to see if Kenny comes— Oh, it's you guys. *(To AMANDA.)* I thought you hated me.

AMANDA. I'm getting over it. We have something to tell you.

KENNY. We told Grandma about you leaving home. She contacted Child and Protective Services.

MARTIN. What? Why would you do that?

AMANDA. Because we care about you. It was wrong to keep this a secret.

MARTIN. I can't believe you guys ratted on me.

KENNY. I know, but it's seriously better this way. Grandma and Amanda worked it out so you can live here, with me.

MARTIN. What about Cassie? I can't…be somewhere if she's still—

KENNY. She's going to stay with your aunt in Rapid City. It's all taken care of.

MARTIN. Really? I don't have to go back?

AMANDA. Never.

MARTIN. I'm staying here?

KENNY. Yeah. But you're not getting my room.

MARTIN *(greatly relieved)*. Wow. Thanks, guys. No one's ever…thanks.

(The kids hug, even KENNY for a moment.)

KENNY. The thing is we have to prove there's nothing in this home that will lead you on a dangerous path to destruction.

MARTIN. I suppose that's you?

KENNY. Well, we always knew I was the cool one. But Amanda has this big idea to redo the whole presentation.

AMANDA. We need to show them that Kenny's not just a dropout; I'm not just a loser; and you're worth taking a risk for.

KENNY. We pull an all nighter, which apparently is something people do for school. So, you with us?

MARTIN. I got nowhere else to be.

AMANDA. Let's get to work! *(She pulls CDs out of her bag.)*

KENNY. We really don't talk, do we?

MARTIN. Not so much. But we could start.

KENNY. Yeah.

MARTIN. I think Grandma Two Hawks has some "Oprah" on tape. *(He shoves KENNY, friends again.)*

(GRANDMA enters. She smiles at her kids.)

MARTIN. Thanks, Grandma. I thought you had tickets to Clay Aiken at the casino tonight?

GRANDMA TWO HAWKS. Can't walk out on my team. Come on, dinner first. Then we work 'til it's done.

(The kids happily follow her out.)

SCENE SIX

(School stage, Monday morning. GRANDMA, MARTIN, KENNY and AMANDA enter and wait at the side of the stage. KENNY mugs for the audience, MARTIN looks serious, and AMANDA is summoning all of her courage.)

MARTIN *(to AMANDA)*. You want me to introduce us?

AMANDA. No, I'm OK.

(MARTIN squeezes her hand, KENNY punches her affectionately in the shoulder.)

KENNY. Don't trip.

(AMANDA smiles and turns to lead them to the center of the stage and…trips. KENNY and MARTIN rush forward and grab each of her arms to save her.)

MARTIN. Kenny!

KENNY. I told her NOT to trip.

(AMANDA straightens herself and gets to the center of the stage.

For a moment we see beige fight to take over AMANDA again, but she battles it back. She address the audience.)

AMANDA. Hey, everyone. I'm Amanda Smith…and I'm a klutz. That's part of who I am. And that's what our presentation is all about.

(A soft Lakota round dance starts. Our group starts stepping in a circle as if in a social dance, but alone.)

AMANDA. Your ancestors and their history are important, if it's Lakota at a *wacipi*…

(The group breaks into eight counts of shawl, fancy and traditional dance in their circle. Then continue walking.)

AMANDA. Pioneers or cowboys at a square dance…

(The group does a fun square dance sequence together. AMANDA and MARTIN as a couple. KENNY dances with GRANDMA.)

AMANDA. Or maybe they were just regular people who lost themselves to disco on a Saturday night…

(The group switches to a disco strut then into a fun line dance.)

AMANDA. But today we're celebrating our living culture. Who we are, today. Five. Six. Seven. Eight!

(The music changes. It becomes a hybrid of Lakota, disco beats and country fiddle set to a contemporary dance beat.

Each of them does a fun solo that claims who they are. Then the four dance together, blending old movement with new. Their partnerships and friendships emerge through dance. The group comes together into a big dance finish and final disco pose! The lights go black.)

THE END

NOTES

NOTES

NOTES

NOTES

NOTES

NOTES